Lessendina   Bageni   Kabirizi   Tumaini   MIZA

LOOKING FOR MIZA

THE TRUE STORY OF THE MOUNTAIN GORILLA FAMILY WHO RESCUED ONE OF THEIR OWN

Told by JULIANA HATKOFF, ISABELLA HATKOFF, CRAIG HATKOFF, and DR. PAULA KAHUMBU

With photographs by PETER GRESTE

SCHOLASTIC PRESS / NEW YORK

THIS BOOK IS DEDICATED TO THE CHILDREN OF THE DEMOCRATIC REPUBLIC OF CONGO, RWANDA, AND UGANDA AND TO A BETTER FUTURE, WHICH WILL ALWAYS INCLUDE MOUNTAIN GORILLAS.

PRONOUNCIATION GUIDE

Kabirizi	Ka-bee-REE-zi
Lessinjina	Less-in-JEE-na
Mikeno	Mick-EN-o
Mivumbi	Mee-VOOM-bee
Miza	MEE-za
Tumaini	Too-ma-EEN-ee
Virunga	Vee-ROON-gah

Additional photographs © 2008, 2007 by Innocent Mburanumwe [pages 4, 8, 12, 13, 15, 16, 17, 29, 36 (left)]; Willam Deed [pages 20, 25, 28, 32]; Samantha Newport [pages 21, 26]; Paul Taggart [page 22]; Diddy Mwanaki [page 36 (right)]. Map on page 34: Courtesy of Jim McMahon.

Library of Congress Cataloging-in-Publication Data

Hatkoff, Craig.

Looking for Miza: The true story of the mountain gorilla family who rescued one of their own / by Craig Hatkoff, Juliana Hatkoff, Isabella Hatkoff, and Paula Kahumbu;

photographs by Peter Greste.   p. cm.

Includes bibliographical references and index.

1. Gorilla—Behavior—Congo—Juvenile literature. 2. Social behavior in animals—Congo—Juvenile literature. I. Greste, Peter, ill. II. Title.

QL737.P96H39 2009   599.884139096751—dc22   2008009544

ISBN-13: 978-0-545-08540-3/ISBN-10: 0-545-08540-3

10 9 8 7 6 5 4 3 2 1   08 09 10 11 12

Printed in Singapore 46 • First edition, November 2008

Book design by Elizabeth B. Parisi • The text was set in 14.5pt. Adobe Garamond.

The authors would like to thank President William Jefferson Clinton, Archbishop Desmond Tutu, Dr. Richard Leakey, and Anderson Cooper for their support of this project. Special thanks go to Kate Waters, Samantha Newport, Jennifer Rees, and, of course, our mom, Jane Rosenthal.

Dear Friends,

We have had the great privilege of bringing two remarkable true stories about young animals facing great adversity from around the world to readers young and old. Owen, a young Kenyan hippo orphaned during the Asian Tsunami, was raised by a giant tortoise named Mzee. Knut, a young polar bear cub who was abandoned by his mother at birth, was raised for months, night and day, by a zookeeper named Thomas at the Berlin Zoo.

We now have a more urgent story to tell about another young animal in distress: a baby mountain gorilla named Miza who lost her mother in the jungles of the Democratic Republic of Congo. What makes this story difficult is that many mountain gorillas have been killed by poachers, roving militias, and people illegally seeking charcoal from the gorillas' natural habitat. The future of the world's remaining population of 700 mountain gorillas is darkly clouded by a clear and present threat of extinction. While these killings seem utterly senseless, the solutions to saving the mountain gorillas are quite complicated. Yet, solutions and answers are needed.

So to answer a few of our questions and help find solutions, we thought we would ask our friends to see if, together, we could help protect and save the gorillas. So we asked President Bill Clinton and the Clinton Global Initiative if they would help. We also asked Archbishop Desmond Tutu and Dr. Richard Leakey, the famed anthropologist, and his organization WildlifeDirect. Now we hope that you will join us as we try to figure this out together, but we have to do it very quickly since time is running short. With your help, we know we can save these majestic creatures! Miza, her family, and the brave rangers who protect the gorillas, are counting on us. Here is their inspiring, true story.

With love and hope,

Craig Hatkoff   *Juliana Hatkoff*   *Isabella Hatkoff*

ALMOST EVERY DAY several hundred Congolese Rangers patrol the beautiful forests and jungles of Virunga National Park in the Democratic Republic of Congo in Africa. The vast park, which spills over into Rwanda, is home to about 380 mountain gorillas, just over half of the planet's remaining mountain gorilla population. Innocent Mburanumwe and Diddy Mwanaki are two of the brave rangers who have dedicated their lives to protecting and saving these magnificent, endangered animals.

One day in June 2007, Innocent and Diddy received some bad news. A baby mountain gorilla named Miza was missing from her family group. They realized that she might be lost in the forest. Innocent and Diddy knew that if they could find Miza, she would have a chance of survival. However, Innocent and Diddy were not the only ones looking for Miza.

This is Miza. She was born on August 12, 2005.

Miza's father, a fierce silverback named Kabirizi, was already looking for Miza. Miza was less than two years old that June day, and still very dependent on her family. Everyone hoped she would be found quickly.

Kabirizi is the leader of Virunga Park's largest family of mountain gorillas. The family, also know as a troop, lives on the slopes of Mount Mikeno. At the time of Miza's disappearance, Kabirizi was responsible for protecting Miza's entire family of 31 gorillas. Kabirizi became the head of a family in 1998 with a small troop of only 9 gorillas. Each family has but one silverback who must fight and defend his position. Over time, Kabirizi's family grew and grew. It is difficult to hold together such a large family. Kabirizi has become famous among the rangers because of his leadership, skills, and bravery.

Sometimes Innocent and Diddy have to cut paths to follow the gorillas.

Miza stays close to her mother, Lessinjina.

Lessinjina was Miza's mother. Miza would ride on her mother's back, clinging to her hair, or cradled on her front. Miza would try to play tag, bounce on branches, and wrestle with the older juveniles but sometimes Miza's mother would hold her back when the play became too rough. The bond between a mother gorilla and her baby is very strong. Like all baby mountain gorillas, Miza would need her mother's milk for food until the age of three although she was beginning to learn to eat on her own.

Miza tries to eat a bamboo shoot. Gorillas eat roots, flowers, bamboo, and other plants.

One of Kabirizi's jobs is to find feeding areas for his family. Miza and her family spend most of every day moving from place to place on Mount Mikeno, eating, playing, and napping. Kabirizi and the adult females keep a close watch to be sure the group stays together.

At night, Miza's mother would make a nest on the ground. She bent and flattened bushes and small trees into a bowl-shaped nest. Miza slept close to her mother. Bageni and Kayenga, young male gorillas, kept watch. One day, Bageni and Kayenga will leave to become silverbacks of their own families, or may even challenge Kabirizi.

Bageni is last in line as the family moves through the forest.
He barks and growls if strange people or animals approach.

When gorillas feel safe, they play. When they are afraid, they sit and huddle, alert and watchful.

The rangers visit the gorillas almost every day. The gorillas recognize Innocent and Diddy and the other rangers. The rangers make friendly gorilla sounds and never threaten the family. Kabirizi watches the rangers as they take pictures and video, draw nose prints to keep track of who is who, and check to see that the gorillas are healthy. The gorillas sometimes play tricks on the rangers, such as stealing their hats!

One of the rangers' jobs is to protect the gorillas from people who may harm them. People called poachers set traps for other animals that gorillas can get caught in by mistake. Other people illegally cut down the forests to grow food for their families and make charcoal for fuel. And sometimes, visitors to the mountains want to watch the gorillas for a long time. But one hour is the limit so that the gorillas do not catch human diseaseslike measels and the flu. The rangers enforce the laws that protect gorillas and they carry guns in case they need to defend the gorillas from harm.

Mountain gorilla families usually have a peaceful life. That was about to change for Kabirizi and his troop.

Miza's mother, Lessinjina.

When the rangers heard that Miza was missing, they rushed up the mountain from their camp. They could not find Kabirizi and his family. The bamboo forest seemed unnaturally quiet. It was clear that something frightening had happened.

A silverback's protective sense is very strong. Kabirizi had led his family high into the mountains to hide. When they were protected, he left his group and began looking for Miza and Lessinjina. He probably looked in the out-of-the-way feeding areas and in quiet hiding places. We will never know exactly where his search took him.

This is Mount Mikeno in Virunga National Park. It is very cold at the top. Gorillas' long hair keeps them warm.

A ranger checks the nose print chart to identify a gorilla. The chart shows the unique pattern of each gorilla's nose.

Slowly, Kabirizi's family came out of hiding. Very carefully, the rangers identified them and counted the family members. But little Miza and her mother, Lessinjina, were still missing and Kabirizi had not yet returned. The rangers searched up and down the mountain, making soft, reassuring gorilla noises, but they didn't find a trace of the missing mother and baby.

After several days, Innocent discovered that Kabirizi had returned. His heart raced. But there was no sign of Miza. Then, in the quiet afternoon at nap time, there was a rustle behind a tree. Innocent slowly turned his head and saw a tiny eye looking up at him through the leaves. He leaned in closer and recognized the unmistakable nose print. This little eye belonged to Miza! His heart soared. Kabirizi had found Miza and brought her home.

Sadly, Lessinjina was still missing.

When Kabirizi returns, he is even more protective of his family.

Miza finds comfort with Tumaini and Mivumbi.

Upon her return, Miza was very shy and timid, and she was very, very hungry. She was afraid of the rangers and hid behind the bigger gorillas.

The rangers were worried. Miza needed a protector and teacher. They were happy to see that Tumaini, Miza's big sister, was taking care of Miza. A baby gorilla needs its mother for nourishment and support, and most of the time other family members do not substitute for the mother. But the rangers watched as Tumaini carried Miza around and grunted softly to soothe her. Miza's half brother, Mivumbi, helped Tumaini. When Miza was left alone, she cried. Right away, Tumaini or Mivumbi would pick her up.

But the rangers worried that Miza was not getting enough to eat, because she seemed weak and acted sick. The skin on her hands had turned bright red and had peeled, and her hair was beginning to fall out. She was in pain and started to have difficulty handling the rough bamboo she was trying to eat.

Miza is having a hard time feeding herself.

Innocent asked Dr. Jacques, a gorilla veterinarian, to observe Miza. Dr. Jacques watched her with the family and also watched her try to eat. He had a hard decision to make. Would Miza learn to feed herself so she could become healthy and strong? If not, she would have to go to a hospital for sick and orphaned gorillas.

Dr. Jacques made the call: "Let her continue to learn to eat the leaves from the forest. There is better medicine for her here with her family than in a gorilla orphanage. She will heal faster if she is here."

Dr. Jacques Iyanya regularly visits the Kabirizi family to check on their health. Here, he makes a special trip to see Miza.

Miza is growing bigger and looks very healthy.

Over the next several weeks, Miza did get better. Innocent and Diddy noticed that Miza had more energy. She was eating a lot more bamboo and her hair was growing back. They saw that Miza could leave Tumaini and Mivumbi for short periods of time. Miza seemed to be gaining confidence and was learning how to trust. She was even starting to let Innocent and Diddy get close to her.

Today, Miza seems to be her happy self. Even without her mother, Lessinjina, who neither Kabirizi, Diddy, nor Innocent were able to find, Miza plays and tumbles with the other young gorillas. She leaps over vines and climbs trees. She even sneaks up on Mivumbi and surprises him.

It is easy to believe that the members of Kabirizi's family are joyful, too. One of their youngest members has survived and is now healthy and happy. Miza will grow up with her family. She will continue to learn from Tumaini and Mivumbi. Kabirizi will carefully watch over his whole troop, but we can be sure that he will always keep an extra-careful eye on Miza, the little, lost gorilla he rescued and brought home.

□

EPILOGUE

What happened to Miza and her mother? Why was Miza missing for so long? We will never know for sure. Lessinjina has not been seen since that day. While Diddy and Innocent continue to look for Lessinjina, Kabirizi seems to know that she will not be found and that he must take care of his family. Lessinjina would never have left her baby alone, so it is likely that she did not survive.

The fact that Miza is thriving is a testament to Kabirizi's power. He found Miza and brought her back to her family. Kabirizi has once again made his family feel secure enough to make room for little Miza. Her recovery is also thanks to Innocent and Diddy and the other rangers who spent so much time looking for Miza, and to Dr. Jacques, who made a difficult decision that seems to have been the right one.

Miza's story is an important reminder. It shows that family care and protection can help one get strong and feel secure. It shows that dedicated people can help endangered animals survive. And it lets us celebrate the safety of one little mountain gorilla, one of the rarest animals on Earth. It also reminds us of the adage, "Seek and ye shall find." And that is the true story of looking for Miza.

THREATS TO MOUNTAIN GORILLAS AND THEIR HABITAT, AND SOLUTIONS

The world's population of mountain gorillas is critically low, with only about 700 mountain gorillas left on the planet. Virunga National Park is the natural habitat for the world's largest concentration of 380 mountain gorillas.

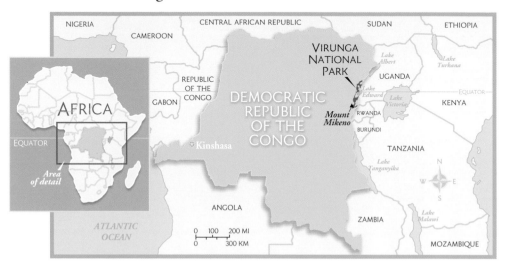

DEFORESTATION

The Democratic Republic of Congo and certain regions in its neighboring countries have been plagued with long-standing ethnic conflict and an unstable political situation. Hundreds of thousands of displaced people have sought refuge in the DRC in camps at the base of the mountains. As more and more people arrive, the camps encroach upon the gorillas' natural habitat. Seeking fuel for cooking, people cut down trees to make charcoal, their primary source. Even though the land in Virunga National Park is protected, there are not enough rangers to police the entire area.

Organizations, including WildlifeDirect, supported by the Owen & Mzee Foundation, are testing portable gas stoves as an alternative cooking method. If these tests are successful, hopefully wide-scale adoption of alternative cooking methods can be implemented and subsidized by the international community and private donations.

HUNTING AND POACHING

Although it is illegal to hunt in the gorilla sector, hunters still set traps and snares to catch animals for food. These traps can seriously injure the gorillas. The rangers and mountain vets try to remove the traps and provide medical assistance to injured gorillas. There are also poachers who try to catch gorillas, especially babies, to sell to private zoos. This is against the law all around the world, but enforcement is difficult and expensive.

There need to be many more rangers to remove snares and traps from the national parks. Wildlife organizations, including WildlifeDirect, collect donations to buy equipment for the rangers and pay their salaries. Increased awareness of the plight of the gorillas will hopefully lead to better international enforcement.

DISEASE

Like humans, mountain gorillas are primates. The 97 percent genetic similarity with humans makes mountain gorillas very vulnerable to diseases such as strep throat, measles, and other common diseases that can be contracted from visitors. That is why visits to the gorillas are limited to one hour. Even the rangers do not stay longer. It is not currently practical for gorillas to get vaccinated.

As tourism increases, it is important that the one-hour visit limit be enforced.

WAR AND CIVIL UNREST

This part of Africa has been plagued by years of war stemming from vicious ethnic conflict and political and economic rivalries. Governments have collapsed after coups and civil wars have raged. While there has been progress in the region, particularly in Rwanda, armed conflict still is rampant. Today there is conflict in the Congo between local militias and government soldiers. The fighting is taking place in the mountains where the gorillas live because the militias have taken control of that sector. It is a very complicated war and the situations change almost daily.

There have been peace talks that may lead to a permanent peace. Enhanced communication and cooperation among the DRC, Rwanda, and Uganda will help establish economic and political solutions. Many people are convinced that the survival of the mountain gorillas depends on establishing peace in the region.

THE DAILY LIFE OF A RANGER

Innocent Mburanumwe and Diddy Mwanaki work for the ICCN (Institut Congolais pour la Conservation de la Nature), the Congolese National Park Authority. They spend almost every day with the gorillas who live in their part of Virunga National Park, checking on the family groups and getting to know the individual gorillas and their personalities and habits. The rangers have a special bond with the gorillas. The gorillas are like family to them.

Innocent is the head of gorilla monitoring in the Mikeno sector of the park. He has worked at Virunga for nine years. His father was one of the first rangers to work with the gorillas. Innocent's brother was a ranger also; he was killed in the line of duty in 1996. Innocent and his wife, Aline, have six children.

Diddy is the head of tourism in the southern sector of Virunga. He has been a ranger for sixteen years. He started to work with the mountain gorillas in the Mikeno sector in 1991. Diddy and his wife, Justine, have six children.

Like all officials who enforce laws, the rangers carry rifles to protect themselves from criminals and warring armies and to protect the gorillas. In addition to monitoring gorillas, the rangers also destroy poachers' traps and stop people from cutting down the forest.

Innocent and Diddy write a blog about their daily activities. You can find it at www.wildlifedirect.org. In the blog, they and other rangers describe the many functions they perform in efforts to protect the gorillas.

Innocent and Family

Diddy's Family

ORGANIZATIONS THAT HELP MOUNTAIN GORILLAS

CGI
CLINTON GLOBAL INITIATIVE
www.clintonglobalinitiave.org

President William J. Clinton launched CGI in 2005 to bring together global leaders and activists to develop and implement solutions to some of the world's most pressing challenges. Members of CGI must make an annual commitment to action. Coauthor Craig Hatkoff is a member of CGI and proposed and sponsored the Mountain Gorilla Project as a 2007 CGI Commitment in partnership with WildlifeDirect, The Desmond Tutu Peace Foundation, Scholastic, and the Owen & Mzee Foundation.

WILDLIFE DIRECT
www.wildlifedirect.org

In 1994, Dr. Richard Leakey, the world-renowned paleontologist and conservationist, became convinced that blogging and other real-time communication via the Internet was the best opportunity for securing a good future for wildlife. He wanted to create a Web site that would allow people who care about wildlife to follow what is happening where the wildlife live. Innocent and Diddy's blog about their work with mountain gorillas is just one of the ongoing blogs on the site.

With major funding coming from the European Union, WildlifeDirect also collects donations from individuals around the world. Every penny goes to the organizations that are protecting wildlife. The ICCN is one of the sponsored agencies. People at WildlifeDirect hope that the monies being raised will eventually "provide a virtual endowment capable of reversing the catastrophic loss of habitat and species."

Dr. Paula Kahumbu is the Head of Conservation, Policy, and Partnerships for WildlifeDirect. Paula is an ecologist who has spent many years studying monkeys and elephants. She is a coauthor of the books about Owen and Mzee, published by Scholastic.

THE OWEN & MZEE FOUNDATION
www.owenandmzee.com

The Owen & Mzee Foundation is a private foundation formed in 2007 by the Hatkoff family, coauthors of the bestselling *Owen & Mzee: The True Story of a Remarkable Friendship.* The foundation makes grants to support educational and environmental causes, activities, initiatives, and organizations. The foundation's first grants were made to WildlifeDirect as part of the 2007 Clinton Global Initiative (CGI) and are being used to support the ICCN Rangers and to establish a test program in the DRC for charcoal cooking alternatives. The foundation will sponsor a range of activities and initiatives for kids to get involved in helping solve the mountain gorilla crisis and other environmental challenges.

ICCN
THE CONGOLESE NATURE CONSERVATION AUTHORITY

There are about 800 Congolese rangers who risk their lives every day to protect the rare species that inhabit the mountains, forests, lakes, and savannas of the spectacular and vast Virunga National Park. These diverse habitats are home to five species of apes, including the critically endangered mountain gorillas, and thousands of other species.

Mivumbi   Bonane   Lessendina   Bageni   Kabirizi